EXPANDING AMERICA

Puerto Rico and the
Spanish-American War

Greg Clinton

New York

Published in 2016 by Cavendish Square Publishing, LLC
243 5th Avenue, Suite 136, New York, NY 10016
Copyright © 2016 by Cavendish Square Publishing, LLC

First Edition

Library of Congress Cataloging-in-Publication Data

Clinton, Greg, author.
Puerto Rico and the Spanish-American War / Greg Clinton.
pages cm. — (Expanding America)
Includes bibliographical references and index.
ISBN 978-1-5026-0972-4 (hardcover) ISBN 978-1-5026-0973-1 (ebook)
1. Spanish-American War, 1898—Puerto Rico—Juvenile literature. 2. Puerto Rico—
History—1898-1952—Juvenile literature. I. Title.
E717.3.C59 2016
972.95'04—dc23

2015025694

Editorial Director: David McNamara
Editor: Andrew Coddington/Kelly Spence
Copy Editor: Rebecca Rohan
Art Director: Jeffrey Talbot
Designer: Amy Greenan/Stephanie Flecha
Senior Production Manager: Jennifer Ryder-Talbot
Production Editor: Renni Johnson
Photo Research: J8 Media

Printed in the United States of America

CONTENTS

INTRODUCTION ... 5
A War and a Turning Point

CHAPTER 1 ... 11
America Flexes Its Muscles

CHAPTER 2 ... 31
Violence in the Media—Spanish War Crimes
and American Competitive Journalism

CHAPTER 3 ... 45
The Germ Theory of History

CHAPTER 4 ... 59
Aftermath, Economies, and
New Forms of Government

CHAPTER 5 ... 71
Long-Term Effects and the Current Situation

CHRONOLOGY ... 82

GLOSSARY ... 86

FURTHER INFORMATION ... 89

BIBLIOGRAPHY ... 91

INDEX ... 94

ABOUT THE AUTHOR ... 96

This artistic depiction shows a naval battle being fought in Manila Bay, Philippines, during the Spanish-American War.

A War and a Turning Point

What leads a nation to war? Do the outcomes of war ever match the reasons for fighting? War seems like a fairly straightforward enterprise, from one perspective. Take a group of people with weapons; threaten, kill, or injure an opposing group of people; and when one group is defeated, settle on a new political arrangement: Who controls the land, the resources, the people? War is played out in simplified form in sports and board games. When a basketball team wins the NBA championship, we understand that one team is victorious, that their "general" (or coach) deserves some credit, and that the "soldiers" (players) were valiant and courageous. Or, two players face off across a chessboard, controlling a medieval army of knights, kings, and queens. The winner is happy; the loser is disappointed. But in the end, everyone goes home.

War is not as simple as sports, and the outcomes are rarely, if ever, so clear. And while we will try to rethink the study of history as a series of wars in this book, there is no doubt that wars have important lasting consequences. In this book, we'll focus on what some might consider an "unimportant" war, a scant two-month clash between the United States and Spain on some isolated islands. Compared to World Wars I and II, the Spanish-American War is a blip on the radar. And yet, as we will discover in this book, that relatively small war had lasting and far-reaching consequences. It set the United States on a course as an **imperial** power, world military force, and global superpower. In the short term, the war expelled the major European interests in the Western Hemisphere, gave control of Puerto Rico and Guam to the United States, and established US military presence in Cuba and the Philippines. In the same year, 1898, the United States also formally **annexed** Hawaii. US territorial expansion had visibly burst outside the borders of the mainland continent.

The War of 1898

The Spanish-American War took place over the course of ten weeks in the summer of 1898. Only thirty years after the Civil War, the Spanish-American War was not as dramatic or momentous as that conflict; it "only" claimed a few thousand American lives. But the conflict with Spain marked the moment when the United States was reborn as a global empire, a transformation that has continued to develop ever since. The war featured historical figures such as future president Theodore Roosevelt and groundbreaking medical researcher Walter Reed. The aftermath left the United States with new territories, new economic opportunities like the completion of the Panama Canal, and new responsibilities to intervene in global affairs. The purpose of this book will be to understand how Cuba, Puerto Rico, and the Philippines fit into the history of the war of 1898.

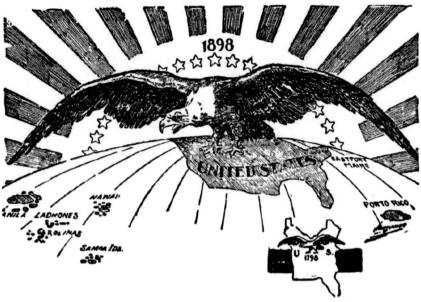

Ten thousand miles from tip to tip.—Philadelphia Press.

This political cartoon shows the eagle, a symbol of the United States, spreading its wings around the globe.

And ultimately, we want to situate these events into the larger story of the United States expanding and gaining confidence, power, and world influence.

The Empire Strikes Back

What does it mean to be an empire? This is an essential concept for understanding the history of the United States, even if you don't hear much about the "American Empire" like you might have heard about the Roman Empire. The United States began life as a collection of colonies, part of the British Empire. In other words, the story we need to tell is of escaping one empire and becoming another. "Empire" means a central authority that governs people, nations, and cultures from a wide area. The Roman Empire, ruled by various Caesars (including the famous Julius Caesar), covered the known world at the time, from the Iberian Peninsula (what is now Spain and Portugal) in the west to India in the east. But the Roman Empire's power was centered in Rome, and Caesar ruled everyone. Britain has ruled over a vast number of colonies, from Asia to Australia to North and South America and Africa.

In many historical examples, like the Roman Empire and the Mogul Empire, an empire had an emperor or an empress. How can a constitutional democracy like the United States be an empire? There isn't an emperor of the United States. There is no central authority; power is checked and balanced among legislative, executive, and judicial branches of government. Despite this form of democratic power, however, the United States has established itself as a powerful form of authority worldwide. The Spanish-American War was the first military exercise of the young United States' imperial project.

The New Colonies

At a certain point, if the United States were to continue its policies of expansion, it would have had to cross an ocean. Starting from the original thirteen colonies, the United States expanded west to the Mississippi, then into the Louisiana Territory and the Western Territories, eventually all the way to the Pacific Ocean, ending its westward expansion at the California coast. As the song "America, the Beautiful" reminds us, the United States sees itself as being blessed by divine grace "from sea to shining sea." But that same "divine grace" and "destiny" that pushed the American **frontier** west to California would eventually project the frontier beyond the sea into faraway lands and continents. With rapidly developing technologies and industries, American businessmen and politicians recognized the

America, the Beautiful

Some people think "America, the Beautiful" is the US national anthem (the anthem is, of course, "The Star Spangled Banner"), but the lyrics to "America, the Beautiful" weren't written until 1895. It was first published as a poem, and the words have changed slightly over time. Many famous musicians have recorded renditions of the tune, including Ray Charles in 1976 and a huge cast of popular country singers in 2001. These performances use the updated 1913 lyrics, which include the famous phrase "from sea to shining sea."

- -

importance of establishing US power in new countries with new markets.

The question remains: Has Puerto Rico played its role as a new economic market for US industries? Or is the status of Puerto Rico and other unincorporated US territories now a political problem? By examining this territory in detail, we can begin to understand the relationship between war, empire, and their long-term consequences.

Young men inspect the terms of recruitment outside the US Army office during the Spanish-American War. Patriotism helped to increase the size of the US military in preparation for the war.

CHAPTER ONE

America Flexes Its Muscles

Looking at a map, Puerto Rico is situated in the Caribbean, a region south of the United States between North and South America. The Caribbean region has two major bodies of water—the Gulf of Mexico and the Caribbean Sea—and features more than seven thousand islands stretching from Cuba to the coast of Venezuela. As of 2015, there are thirteen independent countries among these islands, such as Cuba, Haiti, and Jamaica, but the rest are owned or governed as colonies by mostly European countries. For example, France owns the islands of St. Barts, Guadeloupe, and Martinique. The United States controls Puerto Rico, some of the Virgin Islands, and a small piece of land around Guantanamo Bay, Cuba. For a few decades in the early twentieth century, the United States also occupied Haiti. Why are so many powerful governments—France, England, Spain, and the United States—so interested in controlling these islands?

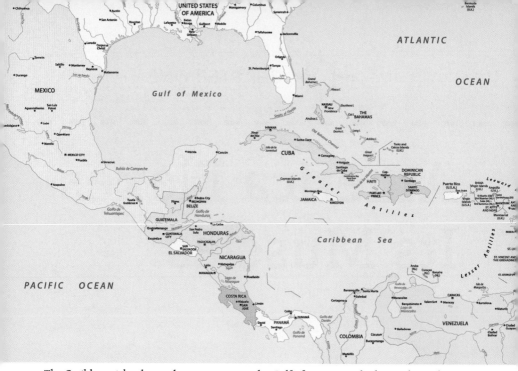

The Caribbean islands acted as a gateway to the Gulf of Mexico and, ultimately, to the future Panama Canal.

Look to the south of the Caribbean islands and you'll notice a strip of land that snakes down from Mexico, growing more and more slender until it touches Colombia, like a tornado touching down on land. Where the land is thinnest is Panama, and in 1914, the United States completed work on a 48-mile (77 kilometer) canal that cut through the land, connecting the Atlantic to the Pacific. Before then, in order to trade with East Asia, a merchant ship from Europe or the East Coast of the United States would have to sail all the way down the coast of South America; go around the southern tip, which is fraught with icy, dangerous waters; sail back up the western coast of the continent; and then cross the wide Pacific Ocean. This took a long time and was very dangerous: a merchant ship might encounter pirates, enemy warships, storms, disease, mutiny, or accidents. The Panama Canal shortened the trip by months and thousands of miles. But it also made the Caribbean a crucial strategic zone. Whoever controlled the Caribbean would control the Gulf of Mexico and the route to the Panama Canal.

French engineers started digging the canal in 1884, fifteen years before the Spanish-American War. The United States took over in 1904 once it had established stricter **dominance** in the region. This shift in power occurred in the years following the Spanish-American War, in 1889. This wide-angle view of the Caribbean helps us keep in mind the strategic and economic stakes in dominating these waters. It also helps us understand why the Caribbean is still a place where global superpowers like the United States, Britain, France, and Spain **exert** enormous influence, and why they are still so interested in the fate of these tiny islands.

Stay Out of the Americas: The Monroe Doctrine of 1823

The other important piece of context for the Spanish-American War is the Monroe Doctrine. By the early nineteenth century, the European nations of France, England, Spain, and Russia had lost their earlier power in the Americas (North and South) but were still interested in regaining it, through economic or military means. By that point, the United States was an established nation, and in 1822 it was joined by independent governments of Mexico, Peru, Colombia, Argentina, and Chile as officially recognized republics.

President James Monroe and his Secretary of State John Quincy Adams decided to send a message to Europe: stay out of the Americas. This is effectively what President Monroe stated in a speech to Congress in 1823. "The American continents," he declared, "by the free and independent condition which they have assumed and maintain, are henceforth not to be considered as subjects for future colonization by any European powers." The United States wouldn't interfere in European wars, but "we should consider any attempt on [Europe's] part to extend their system to any portion of this hemisphere as dangerous to our peace and safety." In other words, *stop trying to interfere in this part of the world, or we'll consider it a threat to our national security.* This ideology has become the backbone for American foreign policy ever since, except that in the twentieth and twenty-first centuries the "national security threat" argument has been extended globally to justify intervening in other countries, such as Vietnam, Korea, Iraq, Afghanistan, and many others.

Although it was established decades before, the Monroe Doctrine helped justify the Spanish-American War and the United States' **acquisition** of Puerto Rico. The Monroe Doctrine merely stated outright what many politicians and businessmen already thought: that Latin America (including the Caribbean islands, Central America, Mexico, and South America) was on US **turf**. The Europeans were no longer welcome. But the United States was interested in this region for two competing reasons: the expansion of slavery and the expansion of industrial **capitalism**.

The United States economy, especially in the Southern states, profited a great deal from slavery. Traders would kidnap people from West Africa and ship them in chains to the Caribbean and the southern United States. There they were sold as slave laborers. Slavery was not **abolished** until 1863, by Abraham Lincoln's famous Emancipation Proclamation. "All persons," he wrote in that document, "held as slaves are, and henceforth shall be free." It took a few years for this to actually be enforced, but by the time the Civil War ended, slavery was officially over. Until then, however, Southern businessmen dreamed of conquering islands like Cuba and Puerto Rico in order to run slave colonies, producing cane sugar, coffee, and other crops for sale on the world market.

On the other hand, many people in the United States were against slavery from the beginning. They saw America's future in industrial capitalism. Instead of **exploiting** people as laborers, they wanted to exploit machines, build better and more automated factories, and invent new technologies of production. This group of politicians and businesspeople saw space and people on the Caribbean Islands, as well as the possibility of connecting the Atlantic and the Pacific, as opportunities for industry rather than agriculture. Those populations could help build factories, and they could work in the factories, producing goods for sale all over the globe.

What Led Up to the War Itself?

By 1898, Spain's colonial empire was shrinking. After leading the charge to colonize the New World—Christopher Columbus was being bankrolled by the Spanish royalty when he made his famous expeditions to the Caribbean—and dominating the region for decades, Spain's hold on power in the Americas faltered.

Setting the Stage for War

The War of 1898, usually known as the Spanish-American War, took place over the course of ten weeks. The established nations at war were, of course, Spain and the United States. There were many other groups involved, however, including Cuban freedom fighters, Puerto Rican **insurgents**, and Filipino freedom fighters. Civilians from Cuba, Puerto Rico, and the Philippines were also involved in the conflict, often coming between the soldiers or supporting one side or the other. For a major international war that had such a lasting impact on global affairs, the Spanish-American War was incredibly brief. By way of contrast, the American Revolutionary War between the American colonies and Great Britain stretched out over about eight years. The American Civil War had lasted almost four. Later in the twentieth century, the Vietnam War would embroil the US military in Southeast Asia for eleven years. The war in Afghanistan began in 2001 and is still being fought as of this writing in 2015.

Part of the reason the conflict didn't last was that Spain was not well prepared to defend its position. Its navy and troops in the Caribbean were far from home and not supported by the local populations. The navy in Manila, Philippines, was unprepared for the strike by American warships and was similarly unsupported by locals. The United States had fresh troops and supplies, and Cuba is a scant 90 miles (149 km) off the coast of Florida, so reinforcements were never far away. The United States was also able to leverage the guidance and local expertise of Cuban, Puerto Rican, and Filipino civilians. US victory was swift and decisive both in the Caribbean and in the Pacific.

Those three locations—Cuba, Puerto Rico, and the Philippines—were Spain's last colonial strongholds. The Spanish empire was in decline and had granted independence to the rest of its formerly vast colonial network in South America and East Asia. On the other hand, in the United States, business was booming at the end of the nineteenth century. Industry was expanding, natural resources were being mined, and there was generally a massive economic upswing (despite a few hiccups). The Transcontinental Railroad had been completed in 1869, and new industries were being developed, including steel, coal, and large-scale manufacturing in factories. This was the so-called "Gilded Age" of America, when it seemed the American economy would never slow its wealth production (but which also came with the creation of a large class of impoverished workers).

Leading the Country: McKinley and Roosevelt

On March 4, 1897, the twenty-fifth US president was **inaugurated**: President William McKinley. William McKinley was born in Ohio in 1843 and won a seat in Congress at the tender age of thirty-four. He quickly achieved success and stayed in the House of Representatives for fourteen years before becoming the governor of Ohio for two terms. While his expertise was in tax law and domestic policy, the major event of his presidency was a foreign affair: the war with Spain. After successfully navigating the war, and increasing America's holdings in the Caribbean and the Pacific, he was elected for a second term in 1900 and took office in 1901. Six months into his second term, he was assassinated by a young **anarchist**. Theodore Roosevelt was sworn in as president on September 14, the day McKinley died from his wounds.

A month after his first inauguration, McKinley had named Roosevelt the assistant secretary of the Navy. Roosevelt was instrumental in planning for the war, before those preparations were even approved by the president or Congress. Roosevelt's peacetime preparation paved the way for a resounding US victory. Theodore "Teddy" Roosevelt was the other major player in the Spanish-American War effort, and his determination, bravery, and drive led him all the way to the White House.

Remember the *Maine*

In January 1898, President McKinley sent the battleship USS *Maine* to Havana's harbor to keep an eye on the Spanish and as a show of potential force. While in the

Teddy Roosevelt, American Progressive

Teddy Roosevelt was born on October 27, 1858, to a wealthy family. To make up for his asthma and other illnesses as a child, Roosevelt dedicated himself to fitness and physical training. This dedication comes out in his glorification of "manly" virtues like hunting, boxing, fighting, courage, and nobility. He attended Harvard College and then Columbia Law School. His first wife, whom he married in 1880 while at law school, was Alice Hathaway Lee. She died on February 14, 1884, the same day that Roosevelt's mother died. He was busy in New York politics at the time, but after the tragedy Roosevelt traveled west to the Dakota Territory to live the life of a cowboy for two years. After his time in the wilderness, he returned to politics, becoming a civil service commissioner and then New York City police commissioner.

Theodore Roosevelt was known as a pioneer for progressive reform in US politics. He established National Forests and championed policies that benefited the poor. According to the National Parks Service, Roosevelt protected some 230,000,000 acres (93,077,698 hectares) of public land during his presidency by creating the US Forest Service, and by establishing fifty-one federal bird reservations, four national game preserves, one hundred fifty national forests, and five national parks. In his own words, Roosevelt describes his outlook on nature:

"We are, as a whole, still in that low state of civilization where we do not understand that it is also vandalism **wantonly** to destroy or to permit the destruction of what is beautiful in nature, whether it be a cliff, a forest, or a species of mammal or bird. Here in the United States we turn our rivers and streams into sewers and dumping grounds, we pollute the air, we destroy forests, and exterminate fishes, birds and mammals—not to speak of vulgarizing charming landscapes with hideous advertisements. But at last it looks as if our people were awakening."

The battleship USS *Maine* exploded in Havana Harbor on February 15, 1898. America immediately accused the Spanish of sabotage.

harbor, on February 15, the ship was rocked by a massive explosion that left 260 American soldiers dead. Immediately, American news outlets began to speculate about Spanish **sabotage**. If Spain had secretly detonated an underwater mine, then the United States would have no choice but to respond with force. A team of American investigators traveled to Cuba and concluded that indeed, the *Maine* was probably destroyed by a mine. The Spanish denied the charges, but public opinion was swayed by sensationalist journalism from outlets such as William Randolph Hearst's *World* and Pulitzer's *Journal* (see "Yellow Journalism" in Chapter 2). The call went up: "Remember the *Maine*! To Hell with Spain!" A declaration of war followed only two months later.

A Quick Victory in the Philippines

The primary targets for the United States were Cuba and the Philippines. Manila, the capital of the Philippines, was taken in spectacular fashion by General George Dewey and the seven ships under his command anchored near Hong Kong. Theodore Roosevelt had prepared Dewey for such a moment by requesting that he keep the ships ready for action and full of fuel. The Congressional declaration of war against Spain was handed to McKinley on April 20, 1898, and Dewey and his ships struck Manila Bay just a week later. It was the first major battle of the war. Dewey was ordered to seek out and destroy (or capture) the Spanish fleet near the Philippines. They were anchored in Manila Bay. Dewey entered the harbor and destroyed the entire fleet—ten ships and approximately four thousand Spanish soldiers—in under seven hours. Six American sailors were wounded during the assault, but Dewey achieved his mission with no loss of American life.

The Cuba Campaign

The target in Cuba was Santiago, a major city on the southeast coast of the island. In response to the American declaration of war, a Spanish fleet had sailed from Europe on its way to the Caribbean, which spurred the United States to engage the battle more quickly. With relatively untrained soldiers but superior supplies, weapons, and naval technology, the Americans were victorious in a few weeks. Soldiers fought bravely on both sides. There were 237 enlisted soldiers killed in the Cuba offensive, along with 21 sailors and marines. Again, compared to later wars that America would fight, and even compared to the Civil War a few decades prior, these casualty numbers were relatively low.

Far more deadly during wartime was disease. Yellow fever, malaria, typhoid, and other tropical diseases killed almost 3,000 US officers and enlisted men in Cuba, Puerto Rico, and the Philippines. Only one-tenth of that number (332 total) were lost to actual battle in those three arenas.

Teddy Roosevelt's Rough Riders

The most famous military exploits in the entire Spanish-American War were those of Teddy Roosevelt and his Rough Riders (who didn't actually ride horses in Cuba). As assistant secretary of the Navy, Roosevelt was able to counsel the need for war against Spain. But when war was actually declared, he promptly resigned his post and asked to be placed in charge of a regiment of volunteer soldiers. He brought in a trusted friend with strong military experience as a commander, and then he solicited applications for his Rough Riders.

According to the **memoir** he wrote after the war, they were overwhelmed with applications from across the country. The **renegade** troop attracted men from Harvard, Yale, and Princeton—well-educated, wealthy, athletic young men from the upper crust of American society looking to prove themselves on the battlefield, much like Roosevelt himself. But they also accepted "rougher" men who had lived for many years as hunters, ranchers, Native fighters, or Civil War veterans, and in some cases, criminals and gamblers. "The life histories of some of the men who joined our regiment," writes Roosevelt, "would make many volumes of thrilling adventure." On the other hand, some of the most famous members of the Rough Riders were "lawmen"—sheriffs in the Wild West who had hunted "desperadoes and law-breakers."

"The temptation is great to go on enumerating man after man who stood pre-eminent, whether as a killer of game, a tamer of horses, or a queller of disorder among his people, or who, mayhap, stood out with a more evil prominence as himself a dangerous man— one given to the taking of life on small provocation, or

Teddy Roosevelt (standing left-center, with boots, suspenders, and round glasses) poses with his Rough Riders after the Battle of San Juan Hill.

one who was ready to earn his living outside the law if the occasion demanded it."

But in 1898, Teddy Roosevelt was eager for glory in battle. He'd spent much of his life hunting, ranching, and cultivating an extremely "masculine" persona. He was highly intelligent; Roosevelt attended Harvard College where he pursued his interest in biology and environmental sciences, as well as his love of history—military history in particular. Despite being from a wealthy family, he had been living "rough" his whole life, waiting for an opportunity to prove himself. In one of his autobiographical essays, Roosevelt famously writes that "every man who has in him any real power of joy in battle knows that he feels it when the wolf begins to rise in his heart; he does not then shrink from blood or sweat or deem that they mar the fight; he revels in them, in the toil, the pain, and the danger, as but setting off the triumph." Teddy Roosevelt became an emblem of action, military bravery, and patriotic determination.

The Rough Riders charged across a valley to take San Juan Hill. They distinguished themselves as **consummate** soldiers, putting themselves in extreme danger. About a quarter of them were killed in the various assaults in Cuba. Roosevelt returned a national hero. The year after the war he was named McKinley's running mate; American voters elected McKinley/Roosevelt in a landslide. When President McKinley was assassinated in 1901, Roosevelt became the twenty-sixth president of the United States.

Roosevelt had always been in favor of American expansion. Expansion was a sign that not only was the American nation strong, but also that its people were strong. Much of what Roosevelt said along these lines could be seen as an expression of white supremacy or racism. In his book *The Rough Riders*, he takes every opportunity to mention that the different racial groups—white, black ("colored"), Native American ("Indian")—worked harmoniously under his command. But his expansionist speeches often included a strong dose of racial reasoning, which was typical for that time period. For example, in 1899 he said, "in every instance the expansion has taken place because the race was a great race. It was a sign and proof of greatness in the expanding nation ..."

The Battle for Puerto Rico

Unlike the hard-fought quest to take Cuba from the Spanish, where hundreds had perished and heroic charges up hills were undertaken, Puerto Rico was a **cinch**. Total casualties: zero officers, three enlisted soldiers. But capturing the island

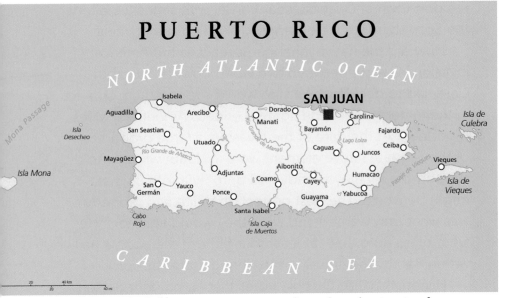

PUERTO RICO

NORTH ATLANTIC OCEAN

CARIBBEAN SEA

A map of the island of Puerto Rico. San Juan is in the northeast, but American forces landed in the southeast near Ponce, hoping to surprise the Spanish.

was vitally important for several reasons: Puerto Rico could be used as a kind of "gateway" to the Gulf of Mexico; it was perfect for industrial and agricultural development; and the inhabitants were tired of Spanish oppression and looking forward to a new, perhaps more free, situation. So on July 21, 1898, a force of 3,314 men left Guantanamo Bay, Cuba, bound for Puerto Rico.

General Nelson Miles led the soldiers. He had announced to the War Department that he would land near San Juan, the capital of Puerto Rico. San Juan is situated on the northeast coast of the island. But the troops actually landed near the city of Ponce on the southeast coast. General Miles had kept his real plans secret, knowing that whatever information he released inside the War Department (information that should have remained secret) might get leaked to the Spanish. He was worried about arriving to find the Spanish soldiers well prepared for defense. Instead, on July 25, the Americans took the port town of Guánica, near Ponce, with almost no effort; the Spanish troops were surprised and fled immediately.

How did the native inhabitants react to the American invasion? Caught between two world powers, the labor class had to decide which side would support them and act in their interest once the fighting ended. As General Miles reported, "At the date of the invasion, a large proportion of the illiterate native element were in doubt whether to support the ills they already had or to fly to others that might be worse. The best protection to life and property was what they wanted and what they would fight for." He went on to note that "at least four-fifths of the people hail with great joy the arrival of the United States troops."

Historian G.J.A. O'Toole notes that "a prudent person would realize that the most important difference between the Spanish and the Americans was that the Americans had all the artillery." In other words, the Americans were a much stronger force. They had fresh and well-trained troops. The Spanish troops on Puerto Rico at the time numbered about 8,000, versus the 3,300 Americans. But the Spanish had no artillery, which are large guns mounted on wheels, that could bombard enemy positions from long range and shoot explosive shells that spread dangerous **shrapnel** from overhead. Artillery was crucial for wearing down defensive positions or defending city walls. Without artillery, the Spanish were at a great disadvantage, even if they commanded more regular soldiers.

The other disadvantage was that the Spanish were losing the war. They had been defeated in Cuba, and Puerto Rico was their last major outpost in the Caribbean. The Spanish were a long way from home, and they faced the home-court strength of the American military. There were two major engagements in the Puerto Rican campaign.

Battles in the Puerto Rican Campaign

Fajardo

The Fajardo **skirmish** was the only battle for Puerto Rico in which the Americans retreated after engaging the Spanish forces. Most of the American forces had been diverted to the southeast by General Miles, against the plan President McKinley and Secretary of War Alger had agreed to. A small expedition did land at Fajardo, near San Juan, in order to try to take that town and hold it before the main bulk of the Americans arrived by land. They landed stealthily and were able to take control of a lighthouse in Cape San Juan. They held their positions, but since they would not be reinforced by General Miles and his battalions, the US sailors ultimately retreated to the sea.

Coamo

The town of Coamo is in the south-central region of the island, a few miles east of the city of Ponce. Spanish and Puerto Rican troops were camped near Coamo when Major-General James H. Wilson and General Oswald H. Ernst led artillery and foot soldiers to surround and destroy the troops and capture the town. After a brief battle, and taking damage from the American artillery, the Spanish surrendered. It was a decisive victory for the Americans and propelled them to a swift victory on the island.

One of the most interesting (and funny) depictions of the battle comes from Richard Harding Davis's book *Notes of a War Correspondent*. Davis was at the skirmish, reporting on the events of the day. In "The Taking of Coamo" he sets the scene:

> "On the morning of the 9th of August, 1898, the
> Sixteenth Pennsylvania Volunteers arrived on the

outskirts of that town. In order to get there they had spent the night in crawling over mountain trails and scrambling through streams and ravines. It was General Wilson's plan that by this flanking night march the Sixteenth Pennsylvania would reach the road leading from Coamo to San Juan in time to cut off the retreat of the Spanish garrison, when General Wilson, with the main body, attacked it from the opposite side."

So far, so good: a typical war report. But Davis is determined to witness the actual surrender of the Spanish troops. So when it seems that General Ernst and his troops are well on their way to entering the town, Davis and a couple of colleagues slip away from the artillery and approach from a different angle. Thinking that Ernst must have already arrived, they wander into town … only to realize that they are the first Americans to arrive!

Looking at the empty streets of Coamo and fearing that the Spanish might be hiding in preparation for an ambush, Davis and his crew hesitate. But their horses are too energetic to stop, so they dash through the center of town. The Spanish are gone, so the reporters "fell off into the arms of the Porto [sic] Ricans."

> "They brought us wine in tin cans, cigars, borne in the aprons and mantillas of their women-folk, and demijohns of native rum. They were abject, trembling, tearful. They made one instantly forget that the moment before he had been extremely frightened.
>
> One of them spoke to me the few words of Spanish with which I had an acquaintance. He told me he was the Alcalde, and that he begged to surrender into my hands the town of Coamo."

Davis accepts the surrender of the town, and for twenty minutes, he is the reigning governor. He uses his twenty minutes to order his friend to drink with the Coamo citizens ("He tells me he carried out my instructions to the letter") and also to "settle one assault and battery" dispute by placing the "chief offender under arrest. At least, I told the official interpreter to inform him that he was under arrest, but as I had no one to guard him he grew tired of being under arrest and went off to celebrate his emancipation from the rule of Spain." In the end, General Wilson rides in heroically, and Davis gives up his "position" as governor of the town.

Davis ends with: "I know that in time the glorious deed of the seven heroes of Coamo, or eight, if you include 'Jimmy,' will be told in song and story. Someone else will write the song. This is the story."

Armistice and the Treaty of Paris

July 17, 1898 marked the surrender of Cuba to the United States. Less than a month later, on August 12, an **armistice**, or truce, was signed by Spanish and American diplomats. The three major colonies—Cuba, Puerto Rico, and the Philippines—were effectively under US control. The official end to the war came on December 10 with the signing of the Treaty of Paris. The terms of the treaty gave the United States control of Puerto Rico and Guam, made Cuba into a United States "protectorate" or pseudo-colony, and purchased the Philippines for $20 million. In 2015 dollars, this would be about $570 million.

Cuban troops camp between battles during the war for Cuban independence from Spain in 1898. The Cuban flag flies proudly above their shelters.

CHAPTER TWO

Violence in the Media—Spanish War Crimes and American Competitive Journalism

t might be an understatement, but in war, everyone starts behaving badly. In some cases, the behavior becomes so extreme that even governments take notice. The generally accepted rules of what constitutes a "just war" (in legal language this is known as *jus ad bellum*, a Latin phrase that translates to "justice in war") can be found in several international treaties. The most famous treaty that covers just war is known as the Geneva Convention, the first of which was signed by major European powers in 1864. But there are many such treaties, including agreements that cover basic rights and fundamental freedoms to which all human beings are entitled (The Universal Declaration of Human Rights), what it means to be a sovereign nation (the Charter of the United Nations), and what should never be done to other people (conventions on torture, the use of weapons of mass destruction and chemical weapons, the treatment of prisoners of war, etc.). Despite the existence of these rules, they are broken all the time. Spanish injustices against Cubans played a major role in motivating the United States to declare war. At the same time, those Spanish injustices were inspired by American violence against Native Americans in previous decades. And as the United States began its own occupation of the Philippines, American forces used torture to suppress the inhabitants of those islands. One episode of violence led to another.

Cuba Revolts Against Spanish Rule

In the nineteenth century, the Caribbean islands had been largely populated by slaves. Large numbers of **indigenous** peoples were killed or driven off the islands by European explorers and settlers in the several centuries following Christopher Columbus's arrival in the Bahamas in 1492. Haiti, a French colony on an island between Cuba and Puerto Rico, had fought successfully for its independence from France at the beginning of the nineteenth century. (The Haitian Revolution was, incidentally, the only successful slave revolt in human history.) Slave populations on other islands were also interested in **self-determination**. Cubans wanted out from under the thumb of Spain, and revolutionary activities boiled over in 1895. Spain had been forced to give some limited autonomy to the Cuban people, but the Cubans wanted full independence. Spain, however, was not ready to give up its most productive and valuable colony in the West. Its response was swift and brutal.

"Weyler the Butcher" and *Reconcentración*

Spain charged General Valeriano Weyler with putting down the rebellion in Cuba. He had become a specialist in quieting violent **dissent** in Spain in his early career, terrorizing rebels in Catalonia into submission. Weyler's tactics against the Cuban rebellion would help motivate the United States to join the war against Spain, but they would also **reverberate** in world history forever as a model for Hitler's treatment of the Jews during World War II.

Weyler found that the rebels were being supported, supplied, and housed by the rural and civilian populations. In February 1896, he decided to separate the rebel fighters from their support base by putting the civilian population into "reconcentration camps." He rounded up entire villages and moved them to guarded prison camps. By 1898, a third of the Cuban population were *reconcentrados.*

The purpose of these camps was to force the rebels out into the open. If the civilian population was under guard, the rebels couldn't hide among them. The plan was rational, but brutal. Approximately four hundred thousand reconcentrados died from starvation and disease. US newspapers, including those owned by Hearst and Pulitzer, portrayed Weyler as "the butcher" of Cuba in cartoons, and they published horrifying images of starvation and death. Photographs of starving camp prisoners circulated in the worldwide press, as well. These images had a strong impact on US popular hatred of the Spanish in the period of time

Spanish prisoners of war being transported to a prison at Guantanamo, Cuba, on June 14, 1901 (Not to be confused with the famous prison at Guantanamo Bay that exists today.)

leading to the decision to go to war. President McKinley was aware of the brutality of the Spanish against the Cubans, and he cited it as an argument in favor of intervention.

A History of Genocide

Genocide is an intentional effort to kill or eradicate an entire group of people. Unfortunately, there have been many such efforts in history. Some evidence suggests that the tactic General Weyler used to suppress the Cuban rebellion—establishing prison camps—was inspired by General William T. Sherman, a decorated US Army officer who led the fight to eradicate Native Americans in the western United States after the conclusion of the Civil War and in the years leading up to the Spanish-American War. Sherman was not alone, however. He was joined in his attempts to kill or imprison all Native Americans by such military men as John Pope, Nelson Miles (who led the campaign in Puerto Rico), future president Ulysses S. Grant, and George Armstrong Custer.

The conflict against Native Americans is known as the American Indian Wars. John Pope declared that "it is my purpose to utterly exterminate the Sioux …" General Sherman was fond of saying that "The only good Indian is a dead Indian" and that his goal was "a racial cleansing of the land." In order to weaken the Native American population further, Sherman and other US military personnel forcibly removed Native groups to land hundreds of miles away from their ancestral homes, to "reservations." These new lands, resource-poor and isolated, were effectively "reconcentration camps" in which thousands died.

Weyler learned from the exploits of the US Army in his approach to the Cubans. It was brutally effective. Only forty years after Weyler, this time in Germany, Adolf Hitler would learn similar lessons from these previous genocides when preparing his "final solution" for the Jews of Europe. When conceiving of his concentration camps during World War II, Hitler "was very interested in the way the Indian population had rapidly declined due to epidemics and starvation when the United States government forced them to live on the reservations."

Expansion is violent, and imperial expansion almost always involves displacing or destroying people who do not support the project of the expanding empire. Weyler faced the Cubans, who wanted democracy for themselves rather than to be subjects to a distant crown. Sherman and the US government faced the Native Americans, who did not want to give up their ancestral lands, their culture, and their lives.

Yellow Journalism

What is the relationship between media and politics? Can news organizations influence politics, and can politicians influence the news? If you turn on the television or look at any Internet news source today, the answer seems obvious: politics and media are tightly tied together. During major political campaigns, millions and sometimes billions of dollars are spent on TV advertisements for each candidate. Politicians routinely appear on programs on CNN, MSNBC, or the Fox News channel. They will even be guests on comedy shows like *The Daily Show with Jon Stewart* or *Between Two Ferns with Zach Galifianakis*. The president of the United States now has an official Twitter account (@POTUS), and the White House runs a Vine account (vine.co/WHVideo) and a Twitter feed (@WhiteHouse). Presidential campaigns are launched on YouTube. The State of the Union Address is live-streamed online, and people discuss it in real time over Twitter and Facebook. From our perspective in the twenty-first century, we can't imagine politics and media more intertwined.

But in the 1890s, the major source of news and information was newspapers. The influence of news media on global political affairs began to intensify in the lead-up to the war with Spain in 1897 and 1898. The major competition in journalism that fueled this intensification took place in New York City between William Randolph Hearst, a brilliant, wealthy young upstart from California who had purchased the *New York Journal* in 1895, and Joseph Pulitzer, owner of the *New York World*. Their rivalry was a little war-within-a-war. Their style of journalism was brash, sensational, and meant to grab the attention of readers at all costs. Pulitzer and Hearst were also interested in changing the world.

William Randolph Hearst— Money, Power, and News

Born in 1863, William Randolph Hearst inherited a massive fortune from his father, California senator and mining magnate George Hearst. After being expelled from Harvard for his raucous pranks (which included sending pots full of excrement to his professors and hosting massive keg parties in Harvard Square), Hearst was looking for something to do. His father had won the *San Francisco Examiner* in a game of chance, so in 1887 the younger Hearst became the newspaper's manager. He decided to make the paper successful at all costs. He spent $8 million of his family's money to hire some of the most famous writers he could find, including Mark Twain (author of *The Adventures of Huckleberry Finn* and *The Adventures of Tom Sawyer*) and Jack London (author of *Call of the Wild*). Hearst pushed his journalists to uncover stories about corporate greed, political corruption, and crime. After making the *Examiner* the most popular paper in San Francisco, he set his sights on New York.

Hearst purchased the *New York Journal* and intended to compete head-to-head with famed newspaperman Joseph Pulitzer. (The Pulitzer Prize, which honors exceptional journalism and literature every year, is named after him.) Pulitzer's *New York World* was the king of New York papers because it emphasized dramatic, sensational stories, bold headlines, engaging pictures, and energetic political opinions that appealed to everyday citizens. Hearst wanted to copy this recipe for success, so he **poached** some of the most talented editors and writers from the *World* and set to work dismantling Pulitzer's dominance.

Hearst was active in politics as well as business, serving in the US House of Representatives. He narrowly lost elections

William Randolph Hearst, the brilliant and ruthless newspaperman who helped to redefine American media and combine journalism with political action

for New York City mayor and New York governor. He went on to construct one of the largest media empires in American history, including dozens of powerful newspapers, radio stations, and movie studios. He built Hearst Castle in San Simeon, California, which has become a national landmark.

Hearst famously battled the release of *Citizen Kane*, a 1941 film by Orson Welles, whose central character is loosely based on Hearst. He sued to get the film banned from theaters, but Welles won out. *Citizen Kane* is routinely listed as the greatest movie of all time by the likes of The American Film Institute, the Sight & Sound poll, and *Time* magazine.

Joseph Pulitzer: A Self-Made Newspaperman

"There is room in this great and growing city for a journal that is not only cheap but bright, not only bright but large, not only large but truly democratic—dedicated to the cause of the people rather than that of purse potentates—devoted more to the news of the New than the Old World; that will expose all fraud and sham; fight all public evils and abuses; that will serve and battle for the people with earnest sincerity."
—from Joseph Pulitzer's *New York Times* obituary

Joseph Pulitzer was born in Hungary in 1847 and emigrated to the United States when he was seventeen years old, in 1864. At that time, immigrants were being encouraged to come to the United States to help fight the Civil War. Pulitzer joined the Union army and fought under General Sheridan for almost a year. He became an American citizen in 1867. He tried his hand at being a lawyer but was unsuccessful. In 1868 he joined the *Westliche Post*, a German-language St. Louis newspaper, as a reporter. In 1879 he made his first newspaper purchase: he bought the *St. Louis Post-Dispatch*. He made the newspaper successful enough that he could afford to buy the *New York World* in 1883.

Joseph Pulitzer, namesake of the Pulitzer Prize, owned the *New York World* and engaged in a bitter rivalry with Hearst over personnel, breaking news, and influence.

News and Emotions Can Shape Politics

What's the most important number for a newspaper? Circulation, or the number of readers. Both Hearst and Pulitzer wanted their newspaper to dominate the market

Puerto Rico and the Spanish-American War

in New York City. In 1883, when Pulitzer purchased the *World*, he began including entertaining content to increase readership, and he kept the price of the paper low (just two cents) so that most people could easily afford it. But more importantly, he began stressing high-interest topics like scandal, crime, and corruption. Hearst honed his skill at this kind of journalism out in California and brought it to New York in 1895. The result was a competition for readers' attention that had notable political consequences.

For one thing, by increasing the sensationalism of news, Pulitzer and Hearst began to rouse the emotions of their readers to a fever pitch. When the *Maine* exploded in Havana's harbor on February 15, 1898, killing 260 American soldiers, the New York papers splashed the story across the front page and screamed for vengeance against Spain. Whether or not the **culprit** really was Spanish sabotage (an investigation in the 1970s concluded that the explosion was most likely caused by an internal explosion—the munitions might have caught fire from the heat of a nearby coal-fired engine, making the explosion an accident) was not really the point. The point was that newspapers could sway public opinion with spectacle and emotion.

Hearst and Pulitzer had set the stage for American intervention by supercharging their reporting. But it wasn't all factual. Their business practices left much room for improvement. Because the two newspapers were so competitive, they often stole material from each other. They had spies in each other's offices, and Hearst and Pulitzer were constantly trying to hire the best writers and editors away from each other. The *World* famously caught the *Journal* red-handed: the *World* ran a small story about the death of a certain Colonel Reflipe W. Thenuz. When the *Journal* **embellished** the story and ran it in their paper, the *World* exposed their journalistic theft by revealing that the original story was a fake. The Colonel's name was an anagram of "we pilfer the nuz." This sort of cutthroat back-and-forth kept the amount of sensationalism and emotion very high leading up to the war.

The Pulitzer Prize

The Pulitzer Prize honors the best American journalism, literature, and musical composition of every year. It was established in 1917 using money from Joseph Pulitzer's estate. The prize, which is given out in twenty-one categories, includes $10,000 in cash. But beyond the money, the Pulitzer is one of the most prestigious awards in writing and composition. Even to be nominated for the Pulitzer is a great honor. Several famous writers and journalists have received more than one Pulitzer Prize, including Robert Frost (four for poetry), William Faulkner (two for fiction), John Updike (two for fiction), and E.O. Wilson (two for nonfiction). A number of novels you might have read in school are Pulitzer winners: *To Kill A Mockingbird* by Harper Lee, *The Old Man and the Sea* by Ernest Hemingway, *Beloved* by Toni Morrison, *The Color Purple* by Alice Walker, and *The Killer Angels* by Michael Shaara.

MAINE EXPLOSION CAUSED BY BOMB OR TORPEDO?

Capt. Sigsbee and Consul-General Lee Are in Doubt---The World Has Sent a Special Tug, With Submarine Divers, to Havana to Find Out---Lee Asks for an Immediate Court of Inquiry---260 Men Dead.

IN A SUPPRESSED DESPATCH TO THE STATE DEPARTMENT, THE CAPTAIN SAYS THE ACCIDENT WAS MADE POSSIBLE BY AN ENEMY

Dr. E. C. Pendleton, Just Arrived from Havana, Says He Overheard Talk There of a Plot to Blow Up the Ship---Capt. Zalinski, the Dynamite Expert, and Other Experts Report to The World that the Wreck Was Not Accidental---Washington Officials Ready for Vigorous Action if Spanish Responsibility Can Be Shown---Divers to Be Sent Down to Make Careful Examinations.

The front page of the *New York World* after the USS *Maine* exploded near Havana, Cuba. The headline stops just short of calling the explosion sabotage.

Nurses stationed at an emergency hospital at the
Pan-American Exposition in Buffalo, New York, in 1901.

CHAPTER THREE

The Germ Theory of History

History is often studied as a series of wars. What caused the war? Who were the opponents? What did they want, and who won? What were the consequences of the battle, and how many people died? And then … when was the next war?

But looking at history as a succession of wars can be misleading. For one thing, it assumes that large-scale change really only comes about through violence. Also, studying wars tends to focus our attention on leaders—presidents, kings, generals—and less on people who are not "in power." We miss the part of the story that can be told about nonmilitary and even nonpolitical forms of historical change. This chapter will focus on some of those issues, even as we look at a war and its aftermath.

Now that we have a sense of how the large political forces operated to cause the military conflict between the United States and Spain, let's focus on science, labor, and gender. What new ideas arose during this period of US expansion to new climates? What new work had to be done, and who did that work? What was the role of men and of women in these events? Answering these questions will help us get beyond military history and frame the world differently.

Valuing Women's Contribution: Establishing the Army Nurse Corps

Traditionally in the Western world, men have been soldiers and women have stayed at home during war. This is one of the reasons we can't just look at military history: too often military history is only the history of men. The reasons for women being excluded from military service are complex but might include some or all of the following **stereotypes** of females:

- Women are physically weaker than men, so they are not up to the challenges of battle.
- Women are less rational than men, so they won't make good decisions on the battlefield. This stereotype also explains why women wouldn't make good military strategists and so aren't allowed to be generals or officers.
- Women are immoral (they will tempt the men to make poor decisions) and will ruin the discipline that an army needs to succeed.
- Women are not as smart as men.
- Women are needed at home to have babies and raise children.

The above list is a catalog of ideas that many still hold even today, but is as old as most civilizations. Women in the United States were not full citizens at the time of the Spanish-American War. Women couldn't vote in elections until 1920! No woman served in Congress until 1916, and no African-American woman until 1968.

During the American Civil War, thousands of women risked their lives and health to work as nurses, caring for the injured and infected soldiers. About 3,200 women nursed Union soldiers. These women were not paid—their work was entirely volunteer—and when the war ended in 1865, they were dismissed. At the time, the military did not see a need for a permanent, professionalized nursing corps. Despite being ignored (or even taken for granted) by the US military, women signed up to support the troops again in 1898.

Very quickly, it became clear that these nurses, some of whom worked for the newly created American Red Cross, made a huge difference to the war effort. "Skeptics were converted into advocates as the evidence mounted that these dedicated nurses saved lives. No longer would the army think of women nurses as glorified housekeepers and cooks. Now it became clear that without female nurses, proper caregiving was impossible." But despite these efforts, the 1,500 nurses were again dismissed after the war.

This time, though, the army accepted the need for professional military nurses. They established the Army Nursing Corps, in 1901. But before this success for recognizing the importance of women in the army, "opposition came from a number of high-ranking officers, who clamored about the expense and friction that would be generated by separate dormitory, mess, laundry, and toilet facilities for women." These arguments were not founded; nurses had very simple living arrangements at camp. Less publicly, the officers voiced concerns about the women's morality. Already you can see the sexism within these arguments: that women are unnecessary, will cause problems, and are immoral. But the sexism was overcome in this case, and the nursing corps was established, even though women still had to wait another two decades before being allowed to become commissioned officers.

Mosquitoes, Microbes, and World Power: Fighting Yellow Fever

Medicine was undergoing important changes at the beginning of the twentieth century. "Germ theory" was gaining widespread awareness due to the work of Louis Pasteur in France and Robert Koch in Germany. Before germ theory, people thought of disease as being caused by "miasma," or bad air. They observed where disease tended to occur: near swampy areas, or in the poor parts of towns and cities. They reasoned that disease must be coming from the stench and filth in these locations. Thus, the way to combat disease was through sanitation, or through discrimination. Get rid of the poor people who carry disease; get rid of the problem! Middle and upper classes felt superior to the poor working class, and felt that because they were cleaner and more civilized they were less prone to illness. This was not really the case, of course, and Pasteur and Koch helped popularize the idea that disease could be caused by microorganisms called germs. The reason disease flourished in poor neighborhoods was not because the people were less civilized, but often because their water sources mixed with their sewage drains due to a lack of infrastructure, or because they were forced to live in crowded conditions.

The late nineteenth century was an exciting time for medicine. In 1881, Pasteur had developed an anthrax vaccine, and by 1864 he had developed the process of pasteurization, a way of killing bacteria in liquids like milk, beer, and wine, still in use today. His rival in Germany, Robert Koch, had shown in 1882 that tuberculosis (TB) was caused by a certain kind of bacteria. Pasteur had also refined a number of scientific techniques and concepts that led to modern bacteriology. It seemed that every year leading up to the turn of the twentieth century, some new discovery was being made to improve health and to win a battle against the microbial enemy.

So, science was becoming the most important weapon against disease. There were visions of "winning the war against disease," of identifying the causes of every infectious or contagious disease and then developing some kind of preventive mechanism to destroy it. One of the first and most important breakthroughs of this kind occurred in Cuba in the years after the US occupation. By 1901, yellow fever had been eradicated in Havana. This represented a stunning medical victory against a horrifying and deadly disease. It also allowed the United States to complete the Panama Canal, cementing its status as a global power. This history is a history of science and medicine, not necessarily of war.

How did this famous event—the use of scientific medicine to successfully combat yellow fever—come to take place? It involves two central figures: Dr. Carlos Finlay, a Cuban doctor educated in the United States and France, and Dr. Walter Reed, a US Army physician.

In the 1880s, Finlay had returned to Cuba from studying medicine in Philadelphia and Paris and established a medical practice in Havana. There, he set to work publishing papers on a wide range of diseases, but his focus was on yellow fever, a disease that until then had remained a mystery even as it killed thousands in the most gruesome way (black vomit, bleeding from everywhere, etc.). Armies fighting in the tropics—the Caribbean, equatorial regions,

In this painting, Dr. Finlay can be seen wearing a black suit (left) and Dr. Walter Reed is in a white uniform in the center. Dr. Lazear is shown inoculating Dr. James Carroll for yellow fever.

Pacific islands, and other tropical zones—typically lost at least as many soldiers to diseases like yellow fever and malaria as they did to actual battle. So, the military had a vested interest in fighting disease. But tropical disease also affects peaceful communities, weakening economies by sickening or killing workers, or decimating family units. This is the brutal reality of disease: it doesn't care who you are or how innocent, how rich or how poor. It attacks everyone it can.

In 1881, Finlay published a paper that caused major **controversy**. In this paper he made a radical claim that yellow fever was spread through mosquito bites. Until that time, yellow fever was thought to spread through "fomites," or objects that were contaminated with the microbe, like blankets or clothing. This is in fact how notorious diseases like smallpox have been transmitted. But yellow fever is a virus that lives in the gut and salivary glands of a particular kind of mosquito: *aedes aegypti*. This mosquito—only the female, who feeds on blood—bites an infected person, ingesting the virus. After a period of two weeks, the virus has multiplied in the mosquito's body, enough to migrate to the salivary glands, where it is ready to be injected into the next person the mosquito bites. This is similar to the concept of shared needles: a purely mechanical way of transferring the disease, not any kind of absorption or contagious method. In other words, you can't get yellow fever by sharing a room with an infected person. Only if a mosquito bites the infected person and then two weeks later bites you, will you be exposed.

Finlay's research had problems: his experiments weren't scientifically sound, so many doctors didn't believe his theory of yellow fever and continued to believe that it was contagious or that it was somehow related to fomites. Walter Reed and his team, after twenty years, finally proved Finlay's mosquito theory.

Reed and his team made several important contributions to medical science in those few years they spent in Cuba between 1898 and 1902. First, they conducted the proper experiments that helped convince the scientific world that Finlay had been right all those years before, even if his experiments had been flawed. This involved experimenting on healthy human beings. How can you prove that a mosquito transmits the disease between humans? The only way is to get a mosquito to bite someone with yellow fever, and then control its transmission to another healthy human. So Reed and his team set up tents with rooms for infected patients to be bitten, and rooms for healthy subjects to be exposed to the mosquitoes. They solved the problem that Finlay had faced: the mosquito, once it had become infected, had to wait two full weeks before it would be able to infect another host.

They also proved that the fomites theory was false— you couldn't get yellow fever from a blanket or curtain— and that the agent of the disease was not bacteria. It was something much, much smaller that doctors had never detected before. That something was a virus. Microscopes with the power to isolate viruses had not yet been developed, but Reed's team discovered that the agent of the disease could pass through a filter designed to catch anything the size of a bacterium or larger. This discovery was a major scientific advancement.

Reed was able to secure funds for a full-scale trial in which army soldiers and Cuban volunteers agreed to contract yellow fever under controlled conditions, to further prove the link. These men signed a form that explained the high risks involved in the experiment. Amazingly, this had never been done before. At the time, if a doctor had a theory, he would often experiment on people without their knowledge or agreement. Walter Reed felt that it was crucial to inform people of the risks and get their agreement before making them a research subject. Today, that practice is called "informed consent," and it is **mandatory** in the United States. Pushing for informed consent was one of the major contributions Walter Reed made to the human sciences.

Putting the new scientific discoveries into practice saved thousands of lives. In Havana, yellow fever was a constant threat. Because of the fomite theory, Cuban health authorities had spent time and money washing walls and disinfecting furniture, hoping to kill the disease where they thought it spread. Now that the United States controlled Cuba, the new health authorities, led by Major William Crawford Gorgas, switched strategies. They began targeting mosquitoes. Teams of sanitation workers went systematically through Havana spraying oil on standing pools of water (where mosquitoes like to breed), cleaning out rain gutters, covering and sealing public drinking sources, and installing metal screens on windows. By 1901, yellow fever had effectively disappeared from the city entirely. The new strategies worked, and the eradication of yellow fever was one of the most important public health victories of its time.

Major US cities enacted the same policies. They stopped wasting time and money quarantining cities with outbreaks and instead fought the mosquitoes directly. For example, in a proclamation from the Louisiana State Board of Health three years before, the President of the Board had stated:

> "Whereas, Yellow fever has been reported in the town of Wilson, La., it is the duty of the State board of health to proclaim, and it does hereby proclaim, that the State of Louisiana quarantines against that town and the parish of East Feliciana, pending investigation.
>
> Freight and passenger traffic shall be governed by the Atlanta regulations.
>
> No tickets shall be sold by railroads and steamboats from that point for any point in Louisiana."

Entire communities were cut off, and trade suffered enormously. Entire economies were devastated while people waited for the quarantine to lift, and if you tried to jump the quarantine, you might be shot. While state governments didn't entirely give up on quarantine as a defense against yellow fever after 1901, their first reaction was now fumigation and screening. At the beginning of the last major US yellow fever outbreak, in New Orleans in 1905, notes read:

> "Two cases and 2 new foci yesterday. Systematic work of fumigation and screening commenced and progressing smoothly."

And:

> "No new cases, 1 death. Yesterday first simultaneous fumigation. One of cases 2 miles out."

And finally:

> "Eight yellow fever, 2 malaria, including undetermined. Yesterday 14 other fever. Tents arrived today. Both hospitals full. Sulphur exhausted. Expect carload to-morrow. General fumigation Saturday. Personal inspection. All water protected."

Using the new knowledge of mosquitoes, US health authorities managed and defeated yellow fever within their borders and in the new tropical colonies as far as they could. Walter Reed became a national hero. (Dr. Finlay has since become a national hero in Cuba, and Reed himself often gave credit to Finlay for the initial discovery.)

Eradicating Disease Is Almost Impossible

In spite of the heroic efforts of doctors, nurses, and medical test subjects, however, only a single major human disease has been declared to be completely eradicated: smallpox. And that didn't happen until 1980. No one knew in the early twentieth century that getting rid of human disease would be nearly, if not totally, impossible. New science of the time pointed to a future without illness.

On the other hand, major advances were made in the field of medical science. For example, vaccine technology has improved immensely. According to the Centers for Disease Control (CDC), a government agency tasked with national public health projects, a long list of previously widespread diseases are now "very uncommon" in the United States because of vaccines. They include diphtheria, Hepatitis A and B, measles, meningitis, mumps, whooping cough, polio, German measles, and tetanus.

Conclusion: Science Enabled Imperial Expansion

Besides the obvious victory over disease and saving lives in Cuba, Puerto Rico, and the United States, why was all this medical science so important to world history? Answer: the Panama Canal. The Canal was a crucial link between the Atlantic and Pacific Oceans. What used to take months—to move a navy from San Francisco to the Caribbean or back again—now took a couple of weeks. Trade would flourish, and whoever controlled the canal would profit from that trade. But the canal was a disastrously deadly project to complete. The French had begun digging the 48-mile (77 km) waterway in 1881 but were forced to give up because of disease. Up to one-third of their workers died each year from diseases like yellow fever. Once Walter Reed's techniques were implemented in 1904, the US crews lost less than 2 percent. They finished the project in 1914, and the era of US imperial expansion was underway.

During the digging of the Panama Canal, the land was softer than anticipated, and digging caused several landslides that delayed the project.

The Germ Theory of History

A field worker near Ponce, Puerto Rico, uses a machete to cut down sugarcane, which was a major economic industry for the Caribbean islands and those who occupied them.

CHAPTER FOUR

Aftermath, Economies, and New Forms of Government

The aftermath of the official war left America with what it really wanted: new economic opportunities. The Caribbean islands offered new markets to control and new labor forces to exploit. The Philippines was a trickier situation, since there was virtually no local support for American occupation. Before it could be used as a stepping-stone to Asian markets, the Philippines had to be subdued. That project took several years and the deaths of several thousand troops (and hundreds of thousands of Filipinos) to achieve.

Cuban and Puerto Rican Sugar Economies

As a slave colony, Cuba was extraordinarily productive. Spain transformed the island into a sugar production facility. Sugar was becoming a much more important **commodity** in the nineteenth century; US and European demand was skyrocketing. In 1894 and 1895, Cuban plantations produced more than a million tons of sugar for export. Once the rebellion began in earnest, production fell to 232,000 tons (210,000 metric tons) in 1896, and further to 218,000 tons (198,000 t) in 1897. While production actually rose to 315,000 tons (286,000 t) in 1898, the war destroyed or crippled a large segment of the industry in Cuba. In 1900, once the US military had taken control of the island and had a chance to survey the damage, only 102 out of 570 sugar mills were still operational.

Puerto Rico, on the other hand, was moving away from sugar as its main source of income. A growing market for coffee in Europe led Puerto Rican farmers to begin investing in coffee production. By the time the United States invaded in 1898, coffee was planted on 41 percent of the island's cultivated land, while sugarcane only accounted for 15 percent. Coffee was bringing in three times as much revenue as sugar. This arrangement was mainly due to the fact that before the war, Puerto Rico produced goods for the European market as dictated by Spain. The European taste for coffee was strengthening, so Puerto Rico produced more coffee.

After the war, when the United States had assumed control of the country, sugar again became important. Now instead of Spain, the United States was Puerto Rico's major trading partner, and the United States demanded sugar.

Why does this matter to the story? Why should we pay attention to details like this when we study history?

The answer is that economic forces shape the daily lives of ordinary people. Under Spanish rule, Puerto Rican farmers did not have the right to determine their own government as they would in a full democracy, but they did have control over their farmland. When the United States took over, it put into place a series of economic policies that restricted a farmer's ability to compete on the global market. For instance, the United States limited the amount of farmland a person could own, and because Puerto Rico's products were now under the umbrella of the US economy, they would have to pay US taxes when they shipped their crops to other countries. Puerto Rican coffee suddenly became less profitable, and farmers couldn't farm as much land as they had in the past. The United States demanded sugar, so farmers turned back to farming sugarcane.

But US corporations had descended on Puerto Rico and bought up farmland. This meant that instead of owning their own land, farmers were increasingly pressured to join the "workforce," producing goods for corporate owners. In only a decade, Puerto Rico's economy had weakened dramatically, and the country had become totally dependent on US trade. Thousands of people were left without the ability to provide for themselves and their families, and there were declines in the autonomy and material conditions of the average worker. As Martínez-Fernández notes, "prices of food and other essential items shot up and unemployment and poverty became more widespread. Emigration became the only option for tens of thousands of Puerto Ricans in the decades to come." In other words, because of the new economic arrangement, more Puerto Ricans left the island, many of them destined for cities like New York and Miami.

Occupying the Philippines, Suppressing an Independence Movement

How did the Caribbean strategy relate to the Pacific strategy? In other words, why did the United States annex Hawaii in 1898 on their way to occupying the Philippines? What strategic advantages did the United States see in becoming a force in the Far East and Pacific regions?

The answer to these questions is at once simple and complex. The simple answer is that the United States wanted a trade route to Asia. Europeans had access to the Suez Canal in Egypt, which cut their transit to Asia by thousands of miles. If the United States wanted to compete on the global market, they had to have a faster way to move goods to the Far East; sailing south to Cape Horn was too dangerous and too slow. Sailing ships (like clipper ships) in the nineteenth and early twentieth centuries could achieve impressively fast top speeds—the *Cutty Sark* could hit twenty-two knots—but averaged only around five to eight knots on long voyages. They had to contend with weather, a lack of wind, wind blowing in the wrong direction, and other challenges. Traveling at five knots, a ship making the voyage from Boston to Sydney would need about 106 days if it sailed around Cape Horn. Sailing through the Panama Canal made it 82 days. From New York to Tokyo along the southern route took 135 days, but through the Panama Canal the time was cut to 80 days. The fastest British route—through the Suez Canal—would still take more than 92 days at that speed. By cutting through Central America, the United States could compete in emerging Pacific Rim economies against the fastest European shipping routes. This was, after all, the entire reason that Christopher Columbus had set sail for the New World: to find a faster route to Asia.

Trade Routes: Breaking Speed Records with the Panama Canal

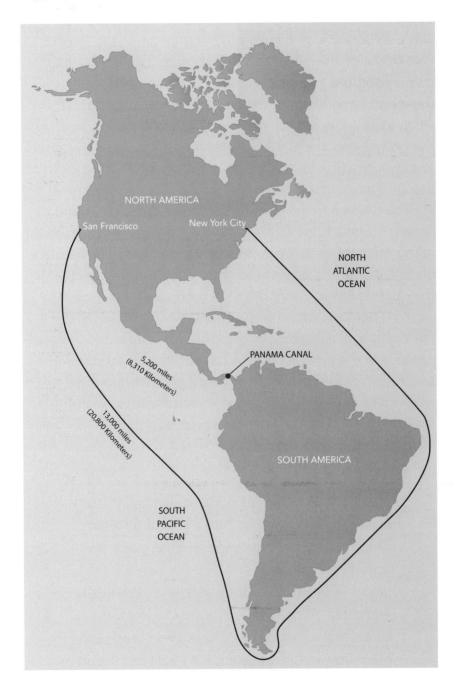

Occupation and Repression

In 1898, while the US military was busy making short work of the Spanish fleet and troops in the Caribbean, the US Navy delivered a devastating blow to Spain in the Pacific. Part of the strategy for the Spanish-American War was to gain a foothold on islands in the East that functioned as a gateway to the Panama crossing, the bridge between the Atlantic and the Pacific. When Spanish rule disappeared in the Philippines, the United States had to decide if it wanted to annex the Philippines or let it become an independent nation. They chose annexation.

There was a fierce debate about this decision in the United States. Some felt that the Filipinos were incapable of ruling themselves, a blatantly racist argument that the black press criticized heavily at the time. Others were sure that if they didn't annex the Philippines then some other country would—perhaps Japan or Germany. At the same time, there was a strong voice of opposition to American imperial projects in the first place. The United States had suffered as a British colony and had won its right to independence; why would it turn around and colonize another land? But commercial and military interests won out.

What happened next was by all accounts a disaster. As historian Stanley Karnow puts it:

> "The US had offered Spain $20 million in the Treaty of Paris to take over. You have a kind of three-way situation: American troops in the Philippines; the Spanish are still there; and then you have a third group—Filipino nationalists commanded by Emilio Aquinaldo. At first, the nationalists welcome the United States, but then you have a very brittle and tense situation around Manila. It's kind of a tinderbox

and nobody knows what's going to happen. Then one night, one of the American soldiers hears a rustle in the bushes, and he shoots and kills one of the Filipinos. Then the whole thing erupts."

Almost immediately, a group of Filipino freedom fighters opposed the US occupation. The leader of the revolutionaries was Emilio Aguinaldo, an upper-class Filipino who had been in **exile** during Spanish rule. When the Americans took over, Aguinaldo returned to the Philippines but was discouraged by the new occupation. As the United States and President McKinley decided to annex the territory, Aguinaldo declared that "my nation cannot remain indifferent in view of such

Filipino freedom fighters who fought against American occupation of the Philippines between 1890 and 1892

a violent and aggressive seizure of a portion of its territory … Thus it is that my government is disposed to open hostilities if the American troops attempt to take forcible possession. Upon their heads will be all the blood which may be shed." What Aguinaldo wanted to do was to draw the Americans into a battle, rather than start one himself. This would make the anger of the Filipino people all the more fierce, if the Americans fired first.

The Water Cure

Controversy has raged over allegations in the past two decades that US forces have used various forms of torture—what former Vice President Dick Cheney refers to as "enhanced interrogation techniques"—including a technique called "waterboarding." This basically mimics the sensation of drowning. Few people seem to remember that controversy over water torture is old news for the United States. Newspapers reported the use of a "water cure" by US soldiers in the Philippines during the occupation. A detainee would be held down, and a pipe or bamboo tube would be forced into his mouth. Then buckets of water would be poured onto his face, going down the tube into his stomach, or up his nose, stopping his ability to breathe. This was repeated until the detainee was bloated with water and struggling for air, at which point the soldiers would force the water out of his body by stepping on his stomach. The majority of the people who were subjected to this treatment died. Several military officials were court-martialed for using this technique, but none were seriously punished.

- - - - - - - - - - - - - - - - - - -

On the night of February 4, 1899, Filipino soldiers provoked a group of Americans into firing on them. Secretary of War Russell Alger wrote that "Alguinado had accomplished that which he had so long conspired to bring about. By an overt act he had succeeded in drawing the fire of our picket.

The Americans had 'fired the first shot.' And this was their signal for assaulting us along the entire line of their works."

The resulting conflict, known as the Philippine-American War, lasted more than three years and resulted in five thousand American casualties, more than eight thousand Filipino combatant deaths, and at least two hundred thousand civilian deaths from violence, disease, or famine. Aguinaldo led his **guerrilla** fighters bravely but was captured by American troops in 1901 and forced to publicly submit to US authorities. The war effort had required almost seventy thousand American troops and several years of bloody conflict full of atrocities on both sides.

The Colonized Becomes the Colonizer: How the United States Repeated the Oppression of Britain

The United States declared its independence from Britain in 1776 with the resounding words:

> "We hold these truths to be self-evident, that all men are created equal, that they are endowed by their Creator with certain unalienable Rights, that among these are Life, Liberty and the pursuit of Happiness. That to secure these rights, Governments are instituted among Men, deriving their just powers from the consent of the governed, That whenever any Form of Government becomes destructive of these ends, it is the Right of the People to alter or to abolish it, and to institute new Government, laying its foundation on such principles and organizing its powers in such form, as to them shall seem most likely to effect their Safety and Happiness."

By defining itself against an oppressive government, the newly independent United States was declaring that it was philosophically and morally opposed to any government that didn't allow for each person's right to live happy and free, or at least to pursue that happiness the way they saw fit. In other words, the basis of the United States was *freedom* and a recognition that the job of the government was to increase freedom, not take it away or destroy it. Yet this is precisely what happened in the Philippines, and a version of these policies is still in place in Puerto Rico.

The Philippine-American War is just one of several military engagements in Asia that the United States has trouble justifying, especially in the hindsight of historical investigation, such as what we are doing now. Is it ever okay for one country to occupy, exploit, repress, and dominate another country? More to the point, can globalization—like the expansion that the United States was pursuing at the end of the nineteenth century—ever occur without this kind of violence?

Guam: A Contested Crossroads

Guam is a small island in a strategic location in the middle of the Pacific Ocean. From Hawaii, Guam is about 4,000 miles (6,437 km) west. From Guam, you can travel 1,600 miles (2,575 km) north to Japan, or 1,500 miles (2,414 km) west to the Philippines. The United States acquired Guam in the Treaty of Paris along with the Philippines, Cuba, and Puerto Rico. It quickly became a staging point for military interests in the Pacific; a shipyard was built there in 1899 and a barracks in 1901. After Aguinaldo's defeat in the Philippine-American War in 1901, he was sent here in exile from his home country.

Guam's indigenous people are known as the Chamarro. Today, there are about 175,000 Chamarro living on Guam, on other Mariana Islands, and in states such as Hawaii,

An F-22 takes off at Anderson Air Force Base in Guam.

California, and Washington. Since the seventeenth century when Guam became a Spanish colony, the Chamarro people have lived under colonial authority of one kind or another.

In 1941, after the attack on Pearl Harbor in Hawaii, the Japanese occupied Guam. They stayed for more than two years, during which they brutalized the populace, subjecting them to physical violence and forcing them to learn and perform Japanese culture. The United States retook the island in 1944 and have administered it as an unincorporated territory ever since. There are two major military installations there that have played a role in US military operations in Asia since World War II. The largest is a naval base in Apra Harbor that hosts more than six thousand troops and seven thousand civilian families, along with retired troops. The Air Force facility on the northeast coast of Guam, Andersen Air Force Base, is the home of the 36th Wing.

The Puerto Rican flag is waved in celebration at a parade.

CHAPTER FIVE

Long-Term Effects and the Current Situation

I n the long run, decisions that were being made about Cuba, Puerto Rico, Guam, and the Philippines were reshaping American national identity. What sort of empire would America become? How should it think about new colonies, and how should it think about itself and its domestic problems? Many of the same questions are being asked even today as the United States is rocked by gun violence, racially charged protests and conflict, and an ongoing military project in the Middle East.

Black Press Reacts to the War

America was on the verge of expanding, and the natural thought was: where to? What new territories would be claimed? But the opposite question is equally interesting and necessary: where from? What was the status of the United States at that moment in history? There were arguments in favor of liberating the Cubans from the "evil oppression" of General Weyler and the Spanish government. How did these arguments hold up next to the state of civil rights in the United States?

In 1898, there was a vibrant black newspaper industry that served the needs of the African-American population throughout the country. The Civil War had ended more than twenty years prior, and slavery had been abolished by President Lincoln's Emancipation Proclamation (and the subsequent Thirteenth Amendment to the Constitution). What had changed in the lives of black people since slavery ended?

Materially, not much. In other words, black people in the United States were impoverished and were not allowed to vote, while lacking education and even basic protections under the law. White people still held all governmental power, even in places in the South where there was a majority black population. Without the right to vote, black citizens were unable to elect leaders of their own. White politicians defended this situation with racist arguments, claiming that black people were not fit to participate in government. Like the attitude toward Native Americans in the West, whites adopted a position known as "white supremacy" that justified not only **disenfranchisement** but outright brutal violence.

The situation in the South was especially dire. Violence against black people was rampant. The Ku Klux Klan organized rallies and mobs to destroy homes and murder black people in order to terrorize the black population into submission. Two especially horrible events took place in 1898: the **lynching** of Postmaster General Frazier Baker and his family on February 22 (two months before the war), and the massacre of black protesters in Wilmington, North Carolina on November 10 (a few months after the war ended). The Baker lynching in particular raised an outcry among the black news media, an outcry that has its echoes in the civil rights movements of the 1960s as well as the increased racial tensions of today.

Frazier Baker had been appointed the Postmaster General of a little town in South Carolina. He had been a schoolteacher. President McKinley appointed a number of black postmasters in the South as a way of giving black citizens, no longer slaves, some positions of authority and pride. Whites in these areas protested. A black person with any authority threatened the feeling of white supremacy. When legal opposition to Baker's appointment failed to remove him from office, a mob attacked his family home in the middle of the night. His house was set on fire. As the family tried to escape the blaze, gunmen opened fire on the family, killing Baker and his two-year-old daughter. Baker's wife and three of his five other children were wounded by gunfire but escaped. No one was ever arrested or prosecuted for the murder.

This was by no means the only lynching; it was only a high-profile example of a larger trend that would continue for decades. Blacks felt harassed and threatened, and were routinely attacked, terrorized, and murdered, especially in the Southern states. So at the moment when US popular opinion was sympathizing with the plight of Cuban prisoners and the violence of the Spanish government against Cuban revolutionaries, the black news media asked: what about us? If we are considering a move toward imperialism, shouldn't we first think about what's happening at home?

The Kansas City *American Citizen* from February 24, 1898, puts it bluntly with a headline that read "Postmaster Baker's Murder and Cuba" and argued that

> "The southern statesmen who plead for Cuba could learn a valuable lesson by looking around their own bloodcurdling confines of butchery ... There is about

as much respect for the Constitution of the United States in the southern states as there is for the Bible in Hades. The atrocious killing of Baker and his baby at the breast of its mother … [was] the work of highly civilized, white, South Carolina American citizens.

… It is the duty of the government to look after the safety of the life of its citizens everywhere. No state, black with treason and anarchy, should be entrusted with human life."

The analogy is powerful: if the atrocities being faced by the Cubans at the hands of Spain are worth fighting a war, then why not the atrocities faced by blacks in the South? Two headlines in the Washington Bee from March 5, 1898, read "Civil Rights First, Cuban Independence Second" and "The Negro Needs Freedom As Much As the Cuban." One editorial pointedly noted that "[the black man's] own brothers, fathers, mothers and indeed his children are shot down as if they were dogs and cattle. Is he living among the brave or is he in the home of his enemies?"

Why should the United States spend so much money on a war for expansion (in the name of liberating Cuba) when it had so many problems back at home? The frustration for blacks was that the government, a white government, did not treat the plight of black people as "a problem." For the most part, the White House and Congress were treating violence against black people as a situation for the states to solve, and not a federal matter.

Who is the real enemy? From the perspective of black Americans, the enemies were white Americans who were prepared to threaten and kill them, and white government, which was allowing the violence to continue. Spain was no enemy, and as urgent as the Cuban situation seemed, it was not more immediate than the lynchings being carried out in their backyards. "Negro's Main Enemy is Southern Lynchers" declared the *Enterprise* out of Nebraska. "The negro still insists that his chief kick is not on the Spaniards but on those fellows who shoot and burn and hang and otherwise kill our fellows in the South. Every negro who bubbles over with patriotic enthusiasm for bleeding Cuba and forgets about the unattained blood of Baker, Lofting, and hundreds of others is a fool and a chump." The *Iowa State Bystander* announced that "White America's Cruelty Equals Spain's."

> "More than 500 colored men and women have been murdered by the American white people in the past 25 years and now they have the audacity to talk about the cruelty of Spain toward the Cubans. There is no half-civilized nation on earth that needs a good hard war more than the United States, and it is high time if there is any such being as an omnipotent just God, for Him to rise and show His hand in behalf of the American Negro."

It is difficult to make sense of racism except to say that it is not entirely rational, but based on a deeply felt worldview. Take the following, from a black newspaper in Minnesota in August, 1898:

> "The Arkansas Democrats held a convention last week and passed resolutions endorsing the war 'now being waged to assist an oppressed people struggling for liberty.' After the adjournment of the convention, some of the delegates returned to their homes and assisted in the lynching of an Afro-American who was charged with stealing a pig."

BILL OF FARE

CUBA STEAK

PORTO RICO PIG

PHILIPPINE FLOATING ISLANDS

SANDWICH ISLANDS

WELL, I HARDLY KNOW WHICH TO TAKE FIRST!

This political cartoon from 1898 shows Uncle Sam (the US) deciding which islands he would like to order for dinner, symbolizing the US deciding which Caribbean islands to gain control of.

This was a dark period of American history that directly influenced the new imperialist project. Part of the justification for occupying the Philippines islands and Hawaii in 1898 was that the native peoples, non-white, were not fit to govern themselves. The pattern we can begin to recognize is that American expansion was not just violent but was founded explicitly on white supremacy. The more disturbing foreign policies since that time harken back to then.

Cuban Independence

After the war, the United States did not allow Cuba to elect its own government right away. The United States didn't annex Cuba the way it did with Puerto Rico, Guam, and the Philippines. This was mainly due to the Teller Amendment to

Why Baseball Is So Popular in Cuba

Roberto Clemente was from Puerto Rico.

Baseball is the most popular sport in Cuba, and it has been since the middle of the nineteenth century. How did baseball make its mark? Already popular in the United States, baseball was imported to Cuba in the 1860s by Cubans who had traveled to the United States for college. Until that time, Cubans had been forced to attend bullfights, in honor of their colonial Spanish government. But the Cubans hated Spain, so they began playing baseball as a way to resist Spanish authority. Because it is such a revered sport in their countries, some of the finest baseball players in Major League Baseball have come from the Caribbean. Notable names include Tony Perez and Jose Canseco (both originally Cuban), Pedro Martinez, Manny Ramirez, David Ortiz, and Sammy Sosa (all from the Dominican Republic), Roberto Clemente, Jorge Posada, Ivan Rodriguez, and Roberto Alomar (all from Puerto Rico). Even Fidel Castro played baseball.

the Congressional Resolution that gave President McKinley approval to go to war against Spain. The Teller Amendment specified that the United States couldn't go to Cuba with the intent "to exercise sovereignty, jurisdiction, or control" over the island. In other words, the United States could only go to war there if they would leave the island alone after it was over. Congress ratified the Teller Amendment in April 1898.

With the Teller Amendment in effect, why did the United States continue to occupy Cuba for years after the war ended? How did they justify this course of action? By 1901, the United States was hard-pressed to explain its continued involvement in Cuba. Instead of simply leaving to allow the newly formed Constitutional Convention of Cuba to draft a new state constitution, Congress proposed a "rider" to the Cuban constitution: the Platt Amendment made it possible for the United States to continue to purchase land in Cuba and to establish military bases and coaling stations. But perhaps most importantly, the Platt Amendment gave the United States the right to intervene in Cuban affairs at any time for "the preservation of Cuban independence, the maintenance of a government adequate for the protection of life, property, and individual liberty ..." Cuba couldn't make any similar agreements with any other country, and they weren't allowed to go into debt. The United States had figured out a way to control Cuba without actually occupying it. The arrangement was imposed until the 1930s when President Franklin D. Roosevelt (Theodore's fifth cousin, also married to Theodore's niece, Eleanor) had the amendment **repealed**.

After decades of Cold War animosity, during which Cuba (which had become a Communist country following the Marxist revolution led by Fidel Castro and Che Guevara) and the United States became bitter enemies, the relationship between the two countries is only now beginning to thaw.

Raúl Castro, president of Cuba, shakes hands with US President Barack Obama at the Summit of the Americas in April 2015.

President Barack Obama announced in December 2014 that normal diplomatic relations would resume. This means that Americans will be allowed to travel to Cuba, use their credit cards there, and import Cuban cigars to the United States. Cuba will also begin to enjoy better trade deals with the United States.

The Status of Puerto Rico

In 2015, Puerto Rico is an unincorporated territory of the United States. This means that it is owned by the United States, but its inhabitants do not have full constitutional rights. The political status of Puerto Rico is an ongoing controversy that began the moment the United States invaded in 1898. Days before the invasion, Spain had granted Puerto Rico a special form of autonomy, or self-rule. When the United States took over, the policies it enacted made the Puerto Rican people less free than under the Spanish autonomy laws. Over time, though, citizens of Puerto Rico have been granted extra rights and privileges, including United States citizenship, although they do not have other rights, such as representation in Congress or the right to vote. This is determined by their status as a territory and not a state.

What defines a state in the United States? A state has its own government: an executive branch (governor), a judicial branch (courts and supreme court), and a legislative branch (state congress). Each US state has its own constitution. In return for allowing the federal government to organize the national economy, set national laws, and collect federal taxes, each state gets a voice in the national government. Each state gets to send representatives to Congress, each state gets to send electoral voters to choose the president and vice president, and each state gets the protection of the US military. Also, people who live in states automatically get to use the federal court system, they have legal rights granted by the US Constitution and the Bill of Rights, and they get to vote for judges, presidents, and Congressional representatives. Citizens of the United States have a say in how their country runs; they have a political voice.

Puerto Rico is not a state, nor are less-famous US territories like the US Virgin Islands, the Northern Mariana Islands, Guam, or American Samoa. Each of these territories has a different set of political circumstances. Puerto Rico's population in 2014 was just over 3.5 million. What rights do these 3.5 million people enjoy?

Since 1917, inhabitants of Puerto Rico have been citizens of the United States. President Woodrow Wilson signed the Jones-Shafroth Act on March 2, 1917. The act established a local Puerto Rican government to be appointed by the president (later revisions to the law allowed the local citizens to elect their local government) and made all inhabitants US citizens, subject to all federal laws. This came with some good news and some bad news for Puerto Rico.

On the plus side, Puerto Ricans took a step toward full US citizenship and all the rights that come with it. Unfortunately, since the island was not a state, the citizens on the island were still cut out of many decisions that would affect them directly, decisions that would be made by the US federal government. Not being from a state, they couldn't—and still can't—send a voting representative to Congress. They can't vote for the president and vice president. They are left out of two of the three main branches of US government because their territory is not "incorporated."

One of the special problems of citizenship became clear almost immediately in 1917. Just two months after the Jones-Shafroth Act, in May, Congress passed a bill authorizing a military draft to support US involvement in World War I. This meant that Puerto Ricans, in becoming US citizens, could now be drafted into the US military and sent to war. Approximately 18,000–20,000 Puerto Rican natives served in World War I. Some viewed this "granting of freedom" as really just a way of **bolstering** the number of soldiers that could be drafted for war.

Puerto Rico in the Twenty-First Century

It is not clear that Puerto Rico should remain an unincorporated territory. But it is not clear what its future should hold. In the twenty-first century, Puerto Rico is a vibrant place with distinct local culture, cuisine, and traditions.

A 2012 **referendum** indicated that many Puerto Ricans do not want to become an independent nation (only around 5 percent voted for this option), but the majority (54 percent) currently favors being admitted as the fifty-first US state. There are at least 4 million Puerto Ricans living in the mainland United States and 3.6 million on the island itself. The island considers itself a distinct country; the people overwhelmingly favor Spanish as opposed to the "official" language, English. President Obama signed a $1 trillion federal government-spending bill in January 2014 that included $2.5 million to run a new referendum on the question of Puerto Rican statehood. Whatever the outcome of that vote, an improved political situation still appears to be many years away.

Chronology

February 16, 1896 General Weyler establishes first of the *reconcentrado* camps; thousands of Cubans are rounded up and imprisoned.

August 26, 1896 Revolution against Spain erupts in the Philippines, setting the stage for American intervention.

March 4, 1897 Inauguration of President William McKinley.

April 6, 1897 Theodore Roosevelt is named assistant secretary of the Navy.

December, 1897 As hundreds of thousands of Cubans died in Spanish concentration camps, President McKinley declares that the United States is ready to forcefully intervene in Cuba.

January 25, 1898 USS *Maine* arrives at Havana on a "friendly visit," but really to begin pressuring the Spanish government with a show of American force.

February 9, 1898 A letter from a Spanish diplomat criticizing President McKinley is published in the *New York Journal*, run by William Randolph Hearst. The letter was intercepted before it reached Spain, and it claimed that

McKinley was weak and that the United States couldn't stand up to Spain. The publication of this letter caused an uproar; American public opinion favored armed intervention against Spain, and this anticipated the public anger at the sinking of the USS *Maine.*

February 15, 1898 After an explosion on the USS *Maine* while it is anchored in Havana Harbor, 268 American soldiers are killed. An investigation by the US military concludes that the ship was the victim of an underwater mine. Americans see this as an act of aggression by Spain. (A subsequent evaluation by scientists in the 1990s decided that the *Maine* probably exploded because of heat from the coal fired engines igniting the ammunition onboard. The Spanish likely had nothing to do with it.)

April 22, 1898 The blockade of Cuba begins, with the US Navy surrounding the major ports and readying an attack on the island.

May 1, 1898 Commodore Dewey destroys the Spanish fleet in Manila Bay, with no American casualties. This triumph is made possible by Theodore Roosevelt's advance planning as the assistant secretary of the Navy.

May 15, 1898 Roosevelt travels to Texas to train with the Rough Riders.

June 22, 1898 The main American force (sixteen thousand troops) land on Cuba to attack the capital city, Santiago de Cuba.

June 24, 1898 The Battle of Las Guásimas, fought between Spanish troops and the Rough Riders.

July 1, 1898 Battle of San Juan Heights and Battle of El Caney. The Rough Riders charge up Kettle Hill, led by Teddy Roosevelt. This cements his status as a national hero and makes it possible for Roosevelt to become vice president a few years later.

July 3, 1898 Spanish navy trapped in harbor try to escape the American blockade and are destroyed.

July 17, 1898 Spain surrenders Cuba to the United States

July 25, 1898 The US military invades Puerto Rico.

August 12, 1898 Truce is signed between Americans and Spanish.

August 13, 1898 Spanish surrender the Philippines.

December 10, 1898 Treaty of Paris is the official end to the Spanish-American War.

February 4, 1899 Fighting starts between US occupation forces in the Philippines and Filipino independence fighters. This is the start of the Philippine War.

March 4, 1901 President McKinley is inaugurated for a second term and Theodore Roosevelt is his new vice president.

September 6, 1901 President McKinley is shot by an anarchist. He will die a week later, making Theodore Roosevelt the twenty-sixth president.

Glossary

abolish To end, make illegal.

acquisition Something taken or gotten.

anarchist A person who believes in dissolving all government.

annex To officially take control of a region of land.

armistice A truce, ceasefire, or agreement to stop fighting.

bolster To support.

capitalism (industrial) A form of economy in which goods are bought and sold; industrial capitalism is based on factory production and industrial technologies.

cinch Easy.

commodity A good or product that can be exchanged for money.

consummate The best kind of.

controversy Public debate.

culprit The person or thing that is responsible for an outcome.

disenfranchisement Losing the right to vote, or not having it.

dissent Resisting the government, disagreeing with those in power.

dominance Power over others.

embellish To make more beautiful or complex; decorate.

exert To try (usually to try hard).

exile Forced to live away from one's home.

exploit To take advantage of.

frontier The outer edge, the limit.

guerrilla A tactic of war in which soldiers use stealth, ambush, and small groups rather than large formations and hierarchies.

imperial Having to do with an empire.

inaugurate To officially declare the beginning of a term.

indigenous People or species that historically come from that region.

insurgent An individual or group that engages in armed uprising against an established power.

lynching A mob attack, usually involving torture and/or murder.

mandatory Required (sometimes by law).

memoir A historical account or biography based on first-hand knowledge; from the French for "memory."

poach To steal.

referendum A popular vote.

renegade Rebel.

repeal To cancel or revoke.

reverberate Echo.

sabotage To intentionally damage something so an opponent will suffer losses.

self-determination The political ability for a group of people to choose their own form of government.

shrapnel Pieces of metal that are propelled outward from an explosion.

skirmish A small fight.

stereotype An attitude that is widely assumed but usually unfair or wrong.

turf Space, land.

wantonly Without regard for reason, moderation, or morals.

Further Information

Books

Freidal, Frank. *The Splendid Little War*. Ithaca, NY: Burford Books, 2002.

Thomas, Evan. *The War Lovers: Roosevelt, Lodge, Hearst, and the Rush to Empire, 1898*. Boston: Little, Brown and Company, 2010.

Zinn, Howard. *A People's History of the United States*. New York: Harper Collins, 2003.

Websites

Crucible of Empire: The Spanish-American War
www.pbs.org/crucible/

This site offers a timeline of the major events before, during, and after the war; photographs of the major figures involved; and newspaper articles and headlines from 1890s newspapers.

The Price of Freedom: Americans at War:
The Spanish American War
amhistory.si.edu/militaryhistory/printable/section.asp?id=7

The online version of a Smithsonian exhibit, this page offers background information and photos of people and artifacts.

Spanish American War
www.history.com/topics/spanish-american-war

Watch a three-minute video about the role of Teddy Roosevelt and the Rough Riders during the Spanish-American War, and more.

Bibliography

Ayala, Cesar J. "Social and Economic Aspects of Sugar
Production in Cuba, 1880-1930." *Latin American
Research Review* 30.1 (1995): 95–124.

Cirillo, Vincent J. *Bullets and Bacilli: The Spanish-American
War and Military Medicine.* New Brunswick, NJ:
Rutgers University Press, 2004.

Davis, R. H. *Notes of a War Correspondent.* Fairfield, IA:
1st World Library - Literary Society, 2004.

Fellman, Michael. *Citizen Sherman: A Life of William
Tecumseh Sherman.* Lawrence, KS: University Press
of Kansas, 1997.

Gould, Lewis L., and Lewis L. Gould. *The Spanish-American
War and President McKinley.* Lawrence, KS: University
Press of Kansas, 1982.

Hofstadter, Richard. *The American Political Tradition:
And the Men Who Made It.* Reissue edition.
New York: Vintage, 1989.

Marks, George P. *The Black Press Views American
Imperialism 1898-1900.* New York: Ayer Co Pub, 1973.

McNeese, Tim. *Remember the Maine!: The Spanish-
American War Begins.* 1st edition. Greensboro, NC:
Morgan Reynolds Publishing, 2001.

Nichols, David A. *Lincoln and the Indians: Civil War Policy and Politics.* 1st edition. Saint Paul, MN: Minnesota Historical Society Press, 2012. Print.

O'Brien, Sara Ashley. "78 Cents on the Dollar: The Facts about the Gender Wage Gap." CNNMoney. April 13, 2015. Accessed June 13, 2015. http://money.cnn.com/2015/04/13/news/economy/equal-pay-day-2015.

O'Toole, G. J. A. *The Spanish War: An American Epic 1898.* New York: W. W. Norton & Company, 1986.

Richardson, James D. *A Compilation of the Messages and Papers of the Presidents – Volume 2, Part 1: James Monroe.* Open Library/FQ Books, 2010.

Roosevelt, Theodore. *The Autobiography of Theodore Roosevelt.* CreateSpace Independent Publishing Platform, 2009.

———. *In the Words of Theodore Roosevelt: Quotations from the Man in the Arena.* Ed. Patricia O'Toole. 1st edition. Ithaca: Cornell University Press, 2012.

———. *The Rough Riders.* Modern Library paperback ed. New York: Modern Library, 1999.

Sarnecky, Mary T. *A History of the U.S. Army Nurse Corps.* 1st edition. Philadelphia: University of Pennsylvania Press, 1999.

Schoonover, Thomas David. *Uncle Sam's War of 1898 and the Origins of Globalization.* Lexington: University Press of Kentucky, 2003.

Toland, John. *Adolf Hitler: The Definitive Biography.* 1st edition. New York: Anchor, 1992.

United States of America. *The Declaration of Independence.* 1776.

"Women in Politics: An Interactive Timeline." *The Washington Post.* http://www.washingtonpost.com/ wp-srv/special/politics/notes-from-the-cracked-ceiling/ timeline/. Accessed May 28, 2015.

"Yellow Fever in the United States." *Public Health Reports (1896-1970)* 20.37 (1905): 1923–1935. http://www.jstor.org/stable/4556075. Accessed May 28, 2015.

"Yellow Fever in the United States from July 1 to September 29, 1898." *Public Health Reports (1896-1970)* 13.39 (1898): 1061. http://www.jstor.org/stable/41440175. Accessed May 28, 2015.

Index

Page numbers in **boldface** are illustrations. Entries in **boldface** are glossary terms.

abolish, 14, 67, 72
acquisition, 14
Aguinaldo, Emilio, 65–66, 68
anarchist, 17
annex, 6, 62, 64–65, 76
armistice, 29
Army Nursing Corps, 47

Baker, Frazier, 72–73
bolster, 81

capitalism (industrial), 14–15
Caribbean region, 11, 13, 59
Chamarro people, 68–69
cinch, 24
Coamo, 27–29
commodity, 60
consummate, 24
controversy, 51, 66, 79
Cuba, 21, 29, 60, 76–78
    present relations with US, 79
    rebellion, 32–34, 60
    relations with Spain, 32–34
culprit, 41

disease, 21, 48–55
disenfranchisement, 72
dissent, 33
dominance, 13, 37

embellish, 41
exert, 13
exile, 65, 68
exploit, 15, 59, 68

Fajardo, 27
Finlay, Carlos, 49, **50**, 51, 54
frontier, 8

Guam, 29, 68–69
guerrilla, 67

Haiti, 11, 32
Hearst, William Randolph, 36–41, **38**

imperial, 6, 8, 35, 56, 64
inaugurate, 17
indigenous, 32, 68
insurgent, 15

Jones-Shafroth Act, 80–81
journalism, 36–37, 40–42, 71–75

lynching, 72–73, 75

mandatory, 52
Manila Bay, 21
McKinley, William, 17, 24, 27, 65, 73
memoir, 22
Miles, Nelson, 25–27
Monroe Doctrine, 13–14

Native Americans, 34–35

Panama Canal, 6, 12–13, 49, 56, 62
Philippine-American War, 66–68
Philippines, 20–21, 29, 59, 64, 76
Platt Amendment, 78
poach, 37
Puerto Rico, 11, 14, 24–29, 60–61, 79–81
Pulitzer, Joseph, 36–37, 39–41, **40**

reconcentration camps, 33
Reed, Walter, 6, 49–52, **50**, 54, 56
referendum, 81
renegade, 22
repeal, 78
reverberate, 33
Roosevelt, Theodore, 6, 17–19, 21–24
Rough Riders, 22–24, **23**

sabotage, 20, 41
San Juan Hill, 24

self-determination, 32
shrapnel, 26
skirmish, 27
slavery, 14–15, 32, 72
Spain, colonial empire of, 15–16
Spanish-American war
    duration, 15–16
    groups involved, 15
    overview, 6, 15–16
    surrender, 29
stereotype, 46

Teller Amendment, 76, 78
Treaty of Paris, 29, 64, 68
turf, 14

United States
    annexation of Hawaii, 6, 62, 76
    formation of, 7, 67
    territorial expansion, 6, 8, 14, 24, 56, 62, 64, 71, 76
USS *Maine*, 17, **20**, 41

wantonly, 19
Weyler, Valeriano, 33, **34**, 71
white supremacy, 72, 76
women, role in war, 46–48

yellow fever, 49–54, 56

About the Author

Greg Clinton is completing a PhD in Cultural Studies at Stony Brook University. His work focuses on the politics of epidemic disease. He teaches courses on cultural criticism, mythology, philosophy, and literature.